W9-AVY-779

Tim Chester is a first rate spiritual physician who knows how to apply the soothing balm of Scripture. For anyone who wants to understand what God is doing in Christian suffering they need look no further. This is a first rate book to be read and re-read.

Melvin Tinker

Author of *Intended for Good: The Providence of God*

Timely and needful. Tim Chester's treatment of a difficult issue is both pastorally sensitive and biblically faithful. A 'go-to' aid for those who find themselves in need of help and counsel when the rod of chastisement strikes. Warmly recommended.

Derek W. H. Thomas

Senior Minister, First Presbyterian Church, Columbia, South Carolina,
Chancellor's Professor, Reformed Theological Seminary,
Teaching Fellow, Ligonier Ministries

As I began to read this book, the Lord brought a period of suffering on our family. It was a wonderful gift to have Tim Chester's warm, honest and hope-filled book in my mind as I engaged with my sin and what our Father was doing. As usual, the author is concerned to be deeply biblical, wrestling with the breadth of the ways the Lord disciplines us. Taking a big view of the Lord's discipline, he manages to loosen it from the moorings of simple punishment, which we know is taken by Christ, in our place, in his suffering on the cross and death. Having set clear water between punishment and discipline, we are shown the scope of Fatherly discipline in conforming our lives to Christ. *God's Discipline* is not an easy read, as I was confronted with my sin, but it helped me to set repentance and growth in the light of a kind, Fatherly love that leads to the Lord disciplining me for my good. This book has opened my eyes to a wider view of God's discipline, and in doing so has set me to further searching the scriptures, and my heart, in a desire to grow in my understanding and appreciation of this aspect of my Father's love. That is the particular joy of *God's Discipline*, it taught me to understand God's discipline, but more, to want to see it, and to desire more of it in my life.

John Hindley
Pastor of Broadgrace Church, Norfolk

How do you know a book is a reservoir of wisdom, encouragement and hope? When virtually every sentence is highlighted, underlined or starred and you've moved on to copying lines onto index cards for the fridge. The Body of Christ *needs* this book. For who among us hasn't struggled to endure and *be trained by* hardship? In this pithy volume, Tim Chester tells us how we can move beyond the pain of life's heartaches to enjoying the harvest of righteousness and peace promised in Hebrews 12. I will be recommending this book to all my biblical counseling colleagues and have ordered a supply for the people I counsel.

Janice M. Cappucci
Certified biblical counselor and author of *Storm Clouds of Blessings: True Stories of Ordinary People Finding Hope and Strength in Times of Trouble*

We believe in God who is sovereign over all things. Therefore we believe in providence, not coincidence. But many of us struggle to understand what the Lord is doing with us as He shapes the ups and downs of our daily lives. 'Why did he allow this?' 'Why didn't that happen when I felt sure it would?' Tim Chester has written a fine, down to earth book tackling such questions. It is full of Biblical common sense and will be helpful to every Christian who reads it. It not only helps us to understand how God trains, corrects and develops us spiritually through life's circumstances, but leaves us genuinely encouraged by our Father's loving purposes.

John Benton

Director for Pastoral Support, Pastors' Academy,
London Seminary Managing Editor, Evangelicals Now

The church of this age shrinks from embracing God's fatherly discipline of His children. This theological reality is seldom taught and even less understood, leaving the church impoverished as a result. Tim Chester's book on this subject is both refreshing and challenging. He explores this crucial biblical teaching with theological precision and pastoral sensitivity. As I read these pages, Tim's writing stirred my heart with the truth that we enjoy a God who so loves us, His children, that He refuses to neglect our souls.

Jason Helopoulos

Associate Pastor, University Reformed Church,
East Lansing, Michigan

In this timely work, Tim Chester raises the stethoscope of Scripture to our ears to expose the hidden heartbeat behind God's discipline, which is love. Every Christian needs to read this book, for it reminds us that God, like a sculptor, sometimes uses jagged tools to chisel away all that is not Christ in us.

Christian George
Associate Professor of Historical Theology,
Curator of the Spurgeon Library, Midwestern Baptist
Theological Seminary, Kansas City, Missouri

God's Discipline

A Word of Encouragement in the Midst of Hardship

Tim Chester

Scripture quotations, unless otherwise indicated, are taken from *THE HOLY BIBLE, NEW INTERNATIONAL VERSION*®, NIV® Copyright © 1973, 1978, 1984, 2011 by Biblica, Inc.™ Used by permission. All rights reserved worldwide.

Scripture quotations marked 'NLT' are taken from *The Holy Bible, New Living Translation*, copyright © 1996. Used by permission of Tyndale House Publishers, Inc., Wheaton, Illinois 60189. All rights reserved.

Scripture quotations marked 'KJV' are taken from the King James Version of the Bible.

Copyright © Tim Chester 2018
paperback ISBN 978-1-5271-0155-5
epub ISBN 978-1-5271-0218-7
mobi ISBN 978-1-5271-0219-4

First published in 2018
by
Christian Focus Publications Ltd,
Geanies House, Fearn, Ross-shire
IV20 1TW, Scotland
www.christianfocus.com
with
Crosslands,
Unit 11, The Old Stables, Westbrook Court,
Sharrow Vale Road, Sheffield, S11 8YZ, England

Cover design by Daniel Van Straaten

Printed and bound by
Bell & Bain, Glasgow.

All rights reserved. No part of this publication may be reproduced, stored in a retrieval system, or transmitted, in any form, by any means, electronic, mechanical, photocopying, recording or otherwise without the prior permission of the publisher or a licence permitting restricted copying. In the U.K. such licences are issued by the Copyright Licensing Agency, Saffron House, 6-10 Kirby Street, London, EC1N 8TS. www.cla.co.uk

Contents

To Matt and Rachel, Phoebe and Ruben

But now, this is what the LORD says —
he who created you, Jacob,
he who formed you, Israel:
'Do not fear, for I have redeemed you;
I have summoned you by name; you are mine.
When you pass through the waters,
I will be with you;
and when you pass through the rivers,
they will not sweep over you.
When you walk through the fire,
you will not be burned;
the flames will not set you ablaze.
For I am the LORD your God,
the Holy One of Israel, your Savior;
I give Egypt for your ransom,
Cush and Seba in your stead.
Since you are precious and honoured in my sight,
and because I love you.'
(Isa. 43:1-4)

Introduction

A 'word of encouragement'. That's how the writer of Hebrews introduces his discussion of God's discipline. My aim is to show how God's discipline is encouraging; how it has the potential to transform our attitude to life and to hardship. We can begin each day with the thought that our Father in heaven has carefully tailored all the events of the coming day to shape us a little bit more into the image of His glorious Son.

The theme of God's discipline overlaps with the issue of suffering because suffering can be something God uses to shape us. The focus of this book, however, is on God's discipline in all its breadth. So it only deals with the issue of suffering as it touches upon the theme of God's discipline. Many other good books have been written to help us understand suffering, both from an apologetic and pastoral perspective.

Suffering can cause people to doubt God's care. But the writer of Hebrews says hardship is the *evidence* of God's fatherly care. God uses suffering to discipline His children. Hebrews 12:1-12 says:

> Therefore, since we are surrounded by such a great cloud of witnesses, let us throw off everything that hinders and the sin that so easily entangles. And let us run with perseverance the race marked out for us, fixing our eyes on Jesus, the pioneer and perfecter of faith. For the joy set before him he endured the cross, scorning its shame, and sat down at the right hand of the throne of God. Consider him who endured such opposition from sinners, so that you will not grow weary and lose heart.
>
> In your struggle against sin, you have not yet resisted to the point of shedding your blood. And have you completely forgotten this word of encouragement that addresses you as a father addresses his son? It says,
>
> 'My son, do not make light of the Lord's discipline,
> and do not lose heart when he rebukes you,
> because the Lord disciplines the one he loves,
> and he chastens everyone he accepts as his son.'
>
> Endure hardship as discipline; God is treating you as his children. For what children are not disciplined by their father? If you are not disciplined — and everyone undergoes discipline — then you are not legitimate,

not true sons and daughters at all. Moreover, we have all had human fathers who disciplined us and we respected them for it. How much more should we submit to the Father of spirits and live! They disciplined us for a little while as they thought best; but God disciplines us for our good, in order that we may share in his holiness. No discipline seems pleasant at the time, but painful. Later on, however, it produces a harvest of righteousness and peace for those who have been trained by it.

Verse 5 says that through His word God addresses you as a father addresses his son. This is true of all of God's word. The Bible is a word to us from our heavenly Father. But the writer has a particular word in mind, Proverbs 3:11-12, which speaks of the way God disciplines those He loves. God is telling us that His discipline is a sign of His love. God chastens everyone He accepts as His son. John Calvin says: 'If no man, at least of prudence and sound judgement, can be found who does not correct his children since they cannot be led to real virtue without discipline, how much less will God, who is the best and wisest father, neglect so necessary a remedy?'[1]

My friend Matt held his five-year-old daughter tightly and inflicted pain on her. I wept as I watched. What kind of father would do such a thing? The answer, as you might have anticipated, is that Matt's daughter Phoebe was ill and needed treatment. She had been diagnosed with a brain tumour and

---

1. John Calvin, *Calvin's Commentaries: Hebrews and 1 & 2 Peter*, trans. William B. Johnston, (Edinburgh: St. Andrew's Press, 1963), p. 191.

was undergoing chemotherapy. The day before, her weakened body had been gripped by fever. Matt was helping the nurses administer her medication. It was causing Phoebe great discomfort. But Matt persisted. Of course he did. This treatment was Phoebe's best chance of survival. His patience and persistence still brings tears to my eyes. Twenty-four hours later Phoebe turned the corner and began to improve (although her battle with cancer continues). Sometimes God our Father holds us tightly in His grip. And what He's doing brings us great discomfort. But far from being a sign of His indifference, it's a sign of His love. With great patience and persistence He is ridding us of the fever of our sin and unbelief.

God treats us in the same way that wise fathers treat their children (Heb. 12:7). 'Know then in your heart that as a man disciplines his son, so the Lord your God disciplines you' (Deut. 8:5). Discipline is a sign that we are part of God's family.

Indeed, our discipline as God's children reflects His discipline of His natural Son, Jesus. This is how the description of God's discipline in Hebrews 12 begins: it begins with Jesus. We are to fix our eyes on Jesus, 'the pioneer and perfecter of faith' (v. 2). Christ is the 'perfecter' of faith because His own faith was 'perfected' through hardship and He becomes 'the pioneer of [our] salvation … through what He suffered' (Heb. 2:10).[2] It was not that Jesus was imperfect in the sense of being sinful, but He was not equipped to be our mediator and priest until He had fully experienced

---

2. I owe this insight to my colleague, Tim Ward.

what it is to be human. So when God disciplines us He is treating us as He treated His Son and equipping us for the roles He has assigned to us. It's a sign we are His children, just as the Son is His child.

Every human father is flawed. And those flaws can affect how we view the discipline of our heavenly Father. You might have had a father who was often selfish, severe, distant or even cruel. So God's discipline makes you think of God as selfish, severe, distant or even cruel. But God's discipline is not selfish or arbitrary. It is carefully designed with your long-term good in mind. It's always an act of love designed to make you more like Jesus.

Or you might have had an indulgent father who rarely disciplined; perhaps your father was desperate to be liked by you. So God's discipline comes as a surprise. It makes God seem by contrast unloving and unlikeable. But actually indulgent parents do not equip their children well to face the world. Their desire to be liked trumps a commitment to the growth of their children. But your heavenly Father is not driven by a desire to be liked by you. Instead He's driven by His love for you. So He is resolutely committed to your growth. His aim is that you enjoy being conformed to the image of His Son. And He carefully, tenderly, lovingly crafts the circumstances of your life to that end.

But the discipline of God raises some important theological and practical questions:
- Does God punish His children?
- What does God's discipline involve?

- Does discipline require a change of direction or repentance from a specific sin?
- Why does God discipline us?
- How should we respond to God's discipline?

But first we start with a story …

1.

Case Study: God's Discipline in the Life of Joseph

The Bible presents us with many case studies in God's discipline, but perhaps the most prominent is that of Joseph. Joseph is the eleventh son of Jacob and the great-grandson of Abraham. Jacob loved him more than any of his brothers because he had been born to him in his old age. So Jacob famously privileged Joseph by giving him an ornate robe. Rather predictably this made Joseph's brothers ill-disposed towards him. Their attitude wasn't helped by Joseph's dream. He dreamt he was a sheaf of corn before which all the other sheaves bowed. He dreamt the sun, moon and stars were bowing before him. Unsurprisingly, this provoked his brothers' jealousy all the more.

One day Joseph's brothers were away, grazing their livestock. Jacob sent Joseph to get news of them.

When they saw Joseph coming, his brothers talked of killing him. Reuben, the eldest, intervened and suggested they merely throw him into a pit. But when a caravan of traders approached, the brothers sold Joseph into slavery. They smeared his robe in animal's blood. When they presented it to their father, Jacob assumed Joseph had been devoured by a ferocious animal.

Meanwhile Joseph was taken to Egypt where he was sold as a slave into the household of Potiphar, one of Pharaoh's officials. The Lord was with Joseph so he prospered and soon Potiphar put him in charge of his household. But Potiphar's wife took a shine to the new handsome slave and tried to seduce him. When he refused, she grabbed his cloak as he fled from the house. Then, with the cloak as 'evidence', she took her revenge. She claimed Joseph would have raped her had her screams not saved her. So Potiphar had Joseph thrown into prison.

Again in prison the Lord was with Joseph and he was given significant responsibilities in the prison. Some time later two of Pharaoh's officials were imprisoned, his cupbearer and his baker. One night they both had dreams. The following morning, with God's help, Joseph interpreted the dreams. The cupbearer would be restored in three days time while the baker would be executed in three days time. And so it proved — three days later the cupbearer was restored and the baker was executed. Joseph implored the cupbearer to remember him when he was restored. But the cupbearer forgot about Joseph.

Two years later, however, the cupbearer had cause to remember Joseph. Pharaoh himself had a dream. Seven sleek, fat cows were standing by the Nile when seven ugly, gaunt cows came out of the river and ate the seven fat cows. This was followed by a second dream. Seven healthy, good ears of corn were swallowed up by seven thin, scorched ears. When the wise men of Egypt could make no sense of the dreams, the cupbearer remembered Joseph and his interpretations. So Joseph was brought from the prison before Pharaoh. The seven fat cows and healthy ears of corn, explained Joseph, represented seven bumper harvests. But these would be followed by seven years of famine, represented by the seven gaunt cows and seven thin ears of corn. Then Joseph offered some advice. Pharaoh should buy up the surplus from the good years and put it in storage. Then food would be available for the seven years of famine, albeit at a price that would enrich Pharaoh. Pharaoh was so impressed with Joseph that he put him in charge and Joseph became the most powerful man in Egypt apart from Pharaoh himself.

The famine extended as far as Joseph's homeland and, when no food was left, Jacob sent Joseph's brothers to Egypt to buy food. In Egypt they bowed before Joseph without recognising him. Joseph, however, recognised them and set them a series of tests to see whether they had changed. In the end he revealed himself to them and invited them, along with his father, to live under his protection in Egypt.

In Genesis 50:15-21, shortly after his father's death, Joseph looks back on his turbulent life:

> When Joseph's brothers saw that their father was dead, they said, 'What if Joseph holds a grudge against us and pays us back for all the wrongs we did to him?' So they sent word to Joseph, saying, 'Your father left these instructions before he died: "This is what you are to say to Joseph: I ask you to forgive your brothers the sins and the wrongs they committed in treating you so badly." Now please forgive the sins of the servants of the God of your father.' When their message came to him, Joseph wept.
>
> His brothers then came and threw themselves down before him. 'We are your slaves,' they said.
>
> But Joseph said to them, 'Don't be afraid. Am I in the place of God? You intended to harm me, but God intended it for good to accomplish what is now being done, the saving of many lives. So then, don't be afraid. I will provide for you and your children.' And he reassured them and spoke kindly to them.

In the introduction I told the story of my friend Matt and his five-year-old daughter Phoebe. Phoebe was diagnosed with a brain tumour on a Tuesday. The very next day I sat in a canteen nursing a cup of cold tea with her mother, Rachel, while Phoebe was undergoing a nine-hour operation to remove the tumour. 'I can see how God might use this to strengthen my faith,' Rachel said. 'But what purpose can there be in this for her? Why must she suffer so I can grow?'

In Genesis 50:20 Joseph says: 'You intended to harm me, but God intended it for good to accomplish what is now being done, the saving of many lives.' Over his life Joseph has been betrayed by his brothers, sold into slavery, falsely imprisoned, abandoned and forgotten. Yet now he can look back on his life with all its puzzles and perplexities, and see that it was worth it. There was a point. There was a bigger purpose and that purpose was the saving of many lives.

'A good and powerful God would and could prevent suffering so, since suffering exists, God cannot exist.' So the argument goes. But this presumes that suffering serves no purpose; that it is pointless. Someone might say, 'I can see that some suffering has purpose. Pain, for example, warns us of illness. But what about the suffering of a five-year-old child like Phoebe? And what purpose is there in so *much* suffering in the world?'

But just because I can't see the point doesn't mean there isn't one. To conclude that there's no point reveals an enormous leap of faith — faith in the ability of our reason to understand life.

Joseph can see that the betrayal, the slavery, the accusations, the injustice, the imprisonment, the abandonment were all worth it. It meant he was in the right place at the right time to save thousands of people from famine. 'You intended to harm me, but God intended it for good to accomplish what is now being done, the saving of many lives.' For Joseph now life makes sense. All that had happened to him had been for a reason. It had made him the man he was — the man to lead Egypt and spare his family. He can trace God's hand in it all.

But this is hindsight. This is not how Joseph experienced his life. He did not know this in advance. He did receive a picture of the future in his dreams. He saw the sheaves of his brothers bowing down to his sheaf. He saw his brothers as stars bowing down to him. But it is fairly cryptic stuff. There is certainly no sense of the saving of many lives.

Instead Joseph experienced his life as a series of setbacks. No doubt he often felt his suffering was pointless.

- How did he feel at the bottom of a pit, looking up at the brothers who had thrown him there? Could he see God's purpose in that? I suspect not.
- How did he feel dragged along behind a camel train, looking back on the brothers who had sold him into slavery? Could he see God's purpose in that? I suspect not.
- How did he feel standing in the slave market, being inspected like a piece of property? Could he see God's purpose in that? I suspect not.
- How did he feel when Potiphar's wife made advances at him? Or when he was falsely accused and thrown into prison? Could he see God's purpose in that? I suspect not.
- How did he feel when the cupbearer forgot about him, after he had interpreted his dream? How did he feel as year after year he languished in prison? Could he see God's purpose in that? I suspect not.

We normally don't get the chance to look back like Joseph to see the point. And in a sense that's the point of the story of Joseph. It is told to show that our suffering has a purpose — even when we can't see that purpose at the time.

So just because we cannot see the point of our suffering doesn't mean there is no point. The Bible also tells the story of Job, a man who lost his property, his children and his health. Job demands answers from God and God does respond. But He does not come to answer Job. Job doesn't get the reassurance that Joseph gets. He can't trace God's purposes in the way that Joseph can. Instead God questions Job: 'Who is this that obscures my plans with words without knowledge? Brace yourself like a man; I will question you, and you shall answer me' (Job 38:2-3). Job did not make the world, nor does he govern it. Job has no idea what the creatures 'behemoth' and 'leviathan' are for. The only sense they make, they make to God. The natural order and the moral order are often incomprehensible to us. God is ultimately inscrutable. So Job doesn't receive answers. He does not get some theory of suffering. But he does receive God: 'Surely I spoke of things I did not understand, things too wonderful for me to know ... My ears had heard of you but now my eyes have seen you. Therefore I despise myself and repent in dust and ashes' (Job 42:3-6).

We are told the story of Joseph so we can be confident God has His purposes in our suffering. But that does not mean we have to work out what those purposes are. That's why we're also told the story of Job. Job teaches us to trust God even when His purposes are unclear. C. S. Lewis writes:

When I lay these questions before God I get no answer. But a rather special sort of 'No answer'. It is not the locked door. It is more like a silent, certainly not uncompassionate, gaze. As though He shook His head not in refusal but waiving the question. Like, 'Peace, child; you don't understand'. Can a mortal ask questions which God finds unanswerable? Quite easily, I should think. All nonsense questions are unanswerable. How many hours are there in a mile? Is yellow square or round? Probably half the questions we ask — half our great theological and metaphysical problems — are like that.[1]

So the message of the story of Joseph is that God is sovereign and so we can trust Him through the ups and downs of life.

But notice how this perspective shapes Joseph's behaviour. The point is not simply that God is in control. The point is that, because God is in control, we can live differently. Joseph's sufferings shape him and refine him.

Here in Genesis 50 Jacob, Joseph's father, has just died. He breathes his last in the final verse of chapter 49 (49:33). Chapter 50 is what happens next. Joseph's brothers fear that with their father out of the way Joseph will use his power to exact revenge on them. Verse 15 says: 'When Joseph's brothers saw that their father was dead, they said, "What if Joseph holds a grudge against us and pays us back for all the wrongs we did to him?"' So they send a message to Joseph.

---

1. C. S. Lewis, *A Grief Observed* (Dent), pp. 58-9.

They tell him that their father had asked Joseph to forgive them. It's not clear whether Jacob really did say this or whether they're making it up.

When Joseph hears this message, he weeps. Again, it's not clear why. Is it because it is a reminder of the wrong that was done to him? Is it because it pains him to think his brothers still fear him? Is it a lament for the broken relationships within the family? Maybe it is all of these things. This is, after all, a man in the midst of bereavement.

What is clear is Joseph's response. Verses 19-21 say:

> But Joseph said to them, 'Don't be afraid. Am I in the place of God? You intended to harm me, but God intended it for good to accomplish what is now being done, the saving of many lives. So then, don't be afraid. I will provide for you and your children.' And he reassured them and spoke kindly to them.

These verses present us with two options. There are two ways we can respond when we suffer or experience injustice.

OPTION 1. WE CAN TAKE GOD'S PLACE

In verse 19 Joseph says: 'Am I in the place of God?' God is in control. He is the Sovereign Lord of the world. But when we don't trust His control we take His place and try to do His job for him. If we take the place of God then we may be:

Domineering
Because we don't trust God's control, we seize control.
We use our power to dominate others, to shape them
to our will.

Manipulative
It is the same root. We don't trust God's control so we
seize control. But, because we don't have authority,
we manipulate instead. It might be emotional mani-
pulation. Or we might nag. We want to control the
situation.

Over-busy
We act as if everything depends on us. And if we think
like that then we will be stressed and busy. We will
try to sort out our problems and maybe also everyone
else's problems. It becomes relentless.

Vengeful
We act as if justice depends on us. If God is not going
to intervene to zap someone then we'll take it out on
them. We might plot revenge or we simply react badly
to that person every time we see them.

Joseph refuses this option — the option of taking
God's place — because he trusts in the purpose of
God. So what does he do instead?

OPTION 2. WE CAN LET GOD BE GOD AND
BE GENEROUS, REASSURING AND KIND
In verses 20-21 Joseph says: '"You intended to harm
me, but God intended it for good to accomplish

what is now being done, the saving of many lives. So then, don't be afraid. I will provide for you and your children." And he reassured them and spoke kindly to them.' Joseph is:

- Generous ('I will provide for you and your children.')
- Reassuring ('Don't be afraid … and he reassured them.')
- Kind ('He … spoke kindly to them.')

We can be generous because our future depends on God and not on us. We can be reassuring because other people's futures depend on God and not on us. We can be kind because our justice depends on God and not on us.

God used Joseph's suffering to save many lives. But perhaps He had another purpose. Would the Joseph who boasted of his dreams to his brothers have said, 'Am I in the place of God?' as he does in verse 19? Would he have reassured his brothers and spoken kindly to them as he does in verse 21? I think not. God had used his sufferings to make him generous, reassuring and kind.

But remember this, too, is hindsight. In the pit Joseph wasn't scoring the progress of his character development. There was no graph on the prison wall charting his month-on-month growth in kindness. The impact of God's discipline is something that at best we see in the rear-view mirror of life. And that means we don't need to identify cause and effect as we go along. What we need to do is trust in the purpose and promises of God.

What did I say to the mother of the five-year-old undergoing brain surgery? Very little most of the time. But I did say this:

> I don't know what God's purposes are. And you don't need to guess. You only need to trust that He has a purpose. And you can trust His love because He has given you His own Son. I don't know what God's purposes are. But I am confident that God will bring you through this terrible time and will lead you safely home to glory.

God is in control and He will lead us home. We can live in the light of God's purpose and God's promises.

2.

Does God Punish His Children?

Does God punish us? No. 'There is now no condemnation for those who are in Christ Jesus' (Rom. 8:1). The work of Christ on the cross is complete. 'It is finished,' He cried (John 19:30). And that means there is nothing left to do. He has paid the price of our sin in full. There is nothing left to pay.

But what about 1 Corinthians 11:29-30? Writing about the abuses of the Lord's Supper in the Corinthian church, Paul says: 'For those who eat and drink without discerning the body of Christ eat and drink judgement on themselves. That is why many among you are weak and sick, and a number of you have fallen asleep.' Members of the church are being judged with illness because of their sin.

Or what about James 5:14-16? James says those who are ill should call for the elders to pray for them. The context suggests these people are ill because of their disregard for the church (James 4:13-17). This is why James calls on them to confess their sins to the representatives of the church 'so that you may be healed' (James 5:16).

Paul, in 1 Corinthians 3:11-15, says our work will be tested by fire. If we have built on the foundation of Christ then we will be rewarded. But if not, then our work will be burned up, although we ourselves will be saved.

How do we make sense of this? On the one hand, God's word clearly says there is no condemnation for those who are in Christ. And the logic of the cross confirms this. God cannot and will not punish our sin twice. He *cannot* because He has already punished our sin at the cross. He *will not* because He loves us as His children. The price paid by Christ was paid in full and so cannot be asked of us again.

On the other hand, the Bible speaks of Christians being judged. It speaks of sin leading to illness.

The answer is that we must make a distinction between punitive (or punishing) judgement and corrective judgement. Condemnation is punitive judgement. Discipline is corrective judgement. Hell is all punitive judgement without any corrective judgement. But God's discipline is all corrective judgement without any punitive judgement. So Christians are sometimes judged, but we are never condemned.

Consider the words used in Hebrews 12 to describe God's discipline of His children. The word 'discipline' is used nine times in Hebrews 12. It's the word Stephen uses to describe Moses being '*educated* in all the wisdom of the Egyptians' (Acts 7:22). It's the word translated 'training' in Ephesians 6:4 when Paul says: 'Fathers, do not exasperate your children; instead, bring them up in the *training* and instruction of the Lord.' In Hebrews 12:6 the writer speaks of chastisement. God 'chastens' His children. Again, it is speaking of corrective judgement. Finally, in verse 11, he speaks of training: 'No discipline seems pleasant at the time, but painful. Later on, however, it produces a harvest of righteousness and peace for those who have been *trained* by it.' All the language here speaks of training, education, formation. Its end product is not condemnation or destruction. Instead we are disciplined 'that we may share in his holiness' (v. 10). It 'produces a harvest of righteousness and peace' (v. 11).

Here's the key point. When we experience God's discipline we are not in the courtroom; we are in the home. 'Endure hardship as discipline', says Hebrews 12:7, 'God is treating you as his children. For what children are not disciplined by their father?'

This matters because it transforms how we view our suffering. Charles Spurgeon says: 'Had any other condition been better for you than the one in which you are, divine love would have put you there.'[1] John

---

1. From Charles H. Spurgeon, *Morning and Evening*, November 11, Evening.

Calvin says: 'Let us therefore remember that no trace of divine love can be seen by us in chastisements unless we are persuaded that the rods with which He punishes our sins are those of the father.'[2] Frederick S. Leahy concludes: 'God does not punish our sins in a legal sense: that he did fully at Calvary. The chastisements he brings upon his people are to be understood as the loving corrections of a merciful and tender-hearted father.'[3]

Here is the mystery. Sometimes a believer and an unbeliever may experience the same suffering. And to one it is the corrective judgement of a loving Father. To the other it is a punishment for sin from a righteous Judge. But in this life, even this judgement is a call to unbelievers to repent. In this life suffering for unbelievers is both punitive and corrective.

Think of it like this: God disciplines His children in love. This means that sometimes unbelievers are caught up in the adversity God allows His children to bear. Suppose God sends a flood that affects a row of houses; He sends this flood to refine a Christian living in one of those houses. Without the gracious work of God's Spirit, her unbelieving neighbours do not and cannot receive it from God as loving discipline. They experience it simply as punishment. It may even harden their hearts against God. But the Christian receives it as an act of loving discipline. Calvin says: 'The elect, as well as the reprobate, are subjected to

---

2. John Calvin, *Hebrews and 1 & 2 Peter*, pp. 190-1.

3. Frederick S. Leahy, *The Hand of God: The Comfort of Having a Sovereign God* (Edinburgh: Banner of Truth, 2006), p. 122.

the temporal punishments which pertain only to the flesh. The difference between the two cases lies solely in the issue; for God converts that which in itself is a token of His wrath into the means of the salvation of His own children.'[4] Or again he says: 'Even if He strikes foreigners and family alike, yet He stretches forth His hand towards the latter to show that He has a particular concern for them.'[5]

A subset of this question is this, *Does God sometimes hide His face from us?* Does He withdraw from us so that we have no sense of His presence and no response to our prayers? The Puritans often spoke in these terms. They had in mind passages like Isaiah 8:17: 'I will wait for the LORD, who is hiding his face from the descendants of Jacob.' But not all Israel were believers. For them God's discipline was a call to faith. Christians, however, are children of God and God does not hide from us. As a father, my discipline of my children was always accompanied by reassurances of my love. Indeed my discipline was itself a sign of my love, as Hebrews 12 reiterates. God comes close to us when He disciplines us. James 5:9 says: 'Don't grumble against each other, brothers and sisters, or you will be judged. The Judge is standing at the door!' James is clearly talking about judgement within the family of God. But this does not involve God being distant. Quite the opposite. He is standing at the door. When God does feel distant, it is not God who is pushing

---

4. John Calvin, *Commentary on the Book of Psalms*, trans. J. Anderson, (Grand Rapids, MI: Eerdmans, 1949), Vol. 3, p. 283.

5. John Calvin, *Hebrews and 1 & 2 Peter*, pp. 190-1.

us away. It is we who are pushing God away. In this situation, God's discipline does not involve Him turning away from us, but inviting us to draw close to Him.

3.

What Does God's Discipline Involve?

Our appreciation of God's discipline is often, I think, too narrow. We jump to thinking of a trip to the head teacher's office. But the word is used in other ways that are also reflected in God's discipline.

Paul uses three images for Christians in 2 Timothy 2:1-7. He's not talking about God's discipline directly, but these portraits of a Christian help us get a bigger picture of what discipline involves. Moreover, Paul is calling Timothy to join him in suffering for Jesus (1:8). So these images are intended to shape how we respond to suffering. Paul speaks of a Christian as a soldier, an athlete and a farmer.

> You then, my son, be strong in the grace that is in Christ Jesus. And the things you have heard me say in the presence of many witnesses entrust to reliable

people who will also be qualified to teach others. Join with me in suffering, like a good soldier of Christ Jesus. No one serving as a soldier gets entangled in civilian affairs, but rather tries to please his commanding officer. Similarly, anyone who competes as an athlete does not receive the victor's crown except by competing according to the rules. ⁶ The hardworking farmer should be the first to receive a share of the crops. Reflect on what I am saying, for the Lord will give you insight into all this.

What does the word 'discipline' mean for each of these people?

For a **soldier** discipline is boots that shine, marching perfectly in step and immediate obedience to your commanding officer. A new recruit will be shouted at a lot. They'll find themselves having to do push-ups or extra duties for misdemeanours. But the result is soldiers who work together under fire. In the same way God is knocking us into shape and preparing us for battle. Without this discipline we would be easy prey for our enemy, the devil.

For an **athlete** discipline is the determination to complete their training regime. Hebrews 12:1 begins with the imagery of an athlete: 'let us throw off everything that hinders and the sin that so easily entangles. And let us run with perseverance the race marked out for us' (See also Hebrews 12:11 and 1 Corinthians 9:24-27). You can't run well if you're wearing a heavy coat or carrying extra pounds round your waist. So we are exhorted to throw them off. But if we don't throw them off, then God may intervene to assist us. Jessica Ennis-Hill won the heptathlon gold medal at the 2012 Olympic Games. She's from Sheffield where I lived for many years and I remember watching a video of her training in my local park. What struck me was a comment from her coach, Toni Minichiello. He said, 'You coach people and the highlight of the session will be … [if] they're sick … Then you kind of feel, yes, I have trained you.'[1] He pushed his athletes hard. Their training hurt. But it produced a gold medal for Ennis-Hill. In the same way God has designed a training regime for you and me. Sometimes He pushes us hard. We may even have moments when we feel like throwing up. But the result is 'the victor's crown'. So God is like a personal trainer getting us into shape.

For a **farmer** discipline means early mornings and late nights. I have a friend who is a shepherd. During the lambing season he is constantly checking on his ewes. Often he has to be up all night to help them give birth. It would be much easier if God only disciplined when we were at our best. But it's often when we're tired or stretched that the sin in our hearts is exposed. Christian growth can be hard work. But before us is the prospect of 'a share in the crops', what Hebrews 12:11 calls 'a harvest of righteousness and peace'.

The English word 'discipline' is related to the word 'disciple' or 'follower'. Jesus trained His disciples by allowing them to follow Him — to watch, to accompany, to replicate His actions. In a similar way, God the Father is like an employer putting together a work-

---

1. http://www.bbc.co.uk/sport/0/olympics/18719849 (5 July 2012).

experience programme. A **trainee** in a new place of work may be given a range of tasks and experiences to equip them for their work. They learn partly through teaching, partly on the job. They're exposed to difficult circumstances so they gain confidence and experience. God the Father has designed a complex and full training package for each believer. Brian Hedges speaks of 'tailor-made trials'.[2] Every circumstance of our life is part of this lifelong development programme. He uses 'all things' for our good and that good is that we become like His Son (Rom. 8:28-29).[3]

There are other important images that help us understand the nature of God's discipline. Jesus says: 'I am the true vine, and my Father is the gardener. He cuts off every branch in me that bears no fruit, while every branch that does bear fruit he prunes so that it will be even more fruitful' (John 15:1-2). Cutting out the branches that bear no fruit is punitive discipline, for they are thrown into the fire (John 15:6). But God's **pruning** is corrective discipline. It produces more fruit. God is trimming back anything that might distract us. He is cutting out the things that might compete for our love. So God the Father is like a gardener pruning us into a fruitful vine.

An academic discipline is a body of knowledge that we acquire through **study**. The word translated 'discipline' in Hebrews 12 is the word used for teaching or

---

2. Brian G. Hedges, *Christ Formed in You: The Power of the Gospel for Personal Change*, (Wapwallopen, PA: Shepherd Press, 2010), p. 220.

3. Adapted from Tim Chester, *You Can Change*, (Wheaton, IL: Crossway, 2010), p. 48.

training a child. As we've noted, it's the word Stephen uses to describe Moses being *educated* in all the wisdom of the Egyptians' (Acts 7:22).

In 1552 five young students were arrested in Lyon as they returned from their studies in Lausanne and imprisoned for their Protestant beliefs. John Calvin wrote to them, assuring them that every effort was being made to secure their release. But ultimately these efforts failed and the young men were executed by the Inquisition. From prison they wrote a letter to the church in Geneva:

> Very dear brothers in Jesus Christ, since you have been informed of our captivity and the fury which drives our enemies to persecute and afflict us, we felt it would be good to let you know of the liberty of our spirit and of the wonderful assistance and consolation which our good Father and Saviour gives us in these dark prison cells …. Further, we are bold to say and affirm that we shall derive more profit in this school of our salvation than has been the case in any place where we have studied, and we testify that this is the true school of the children of God in which they learn more than the disciples of the philosophers ever did in their universities.[4]

The Reformer Martin Luther once gave this following advice to those who aspired to study theology:

> I want you to know how to study theology in the right way. I have practiced this method myself … The method of which I am speaking is the one which the holy

---

4. Cited in Frederick S. Leahy, *The Hand of God*, p. 131.

> king David teaches in Psalm 119 .... Here you will find
> three rules. They are frequently proposed throughout
> the psalm and run thus: *oratio, meditatio, tentatio*
> [prayer, meditation, trials].[5]

Luther had in mind verses like these: 'Before I was afflicted I went astray, but now I obey your word' (Ps. 119:67). 'It was good for me to be afflicted so that I might learn your decrees' (Ps. 119:71). 'I know, LORD, that your laws are righteous, and that in faithfulness you have afflicted me' (Ps. 119:75). It is often trials that move knowledge from our heads and embed it in our hearts.

Or think of God as a **sculptor** shaping you as a person. He's creating a masterpiece because He's shaping you into the image of His Son. But He's not working with inanimate stone. God is working with a human soul. And His tools are not a hammer and chisel, but the circumstances of your life.[6] The Puritan Thomas Watson said, 'God's rod is a pencil to draw Christ's image more lively on us.'[7]

So God uses *all* the circumstances of our lives to shape us into the image of His Son. He uses the good things and the bad things. But His discipline certainly does include suffering. Don Carson says: 'Scanning the narratives of Scripture ... God's discipline may

---

5. Brian G. Hedges, *Christ Formed in You*, p. 223.

6. See Tim Chester, *You Can Pray*, (Nottingham: IVP, 2014), p. 93; and Horatius Bonar, *God's Way of Holiness*, 1864, (Welwyn: Evangelical Press, 1979), pp. 5-6.

7. Thomas Watson, *All Things for Good*, 1663, (Edinburgh: Banner of Truth, 1998), p. 28.

include war, plague, illness, rebuke, ill-defined and rather personal "thorns", bereavement, loss of status, personal opposition, and much else beside.'[8]

Most of these things are also described as being the result of life in the fallen world, the evil of other people or the work of Satan. Paul describes his 'thorn in the flesh' as both 'a messenger of Satan' and a gift from God (2 Cor. 12:7). This is the mystery of divine providence. God works through evil to achieve His good purposes. This truth helps us in two ways:

1. Suffering is evil. First, we don't have to pretend that bad things are good. 'No discipline seems pleasant at the time, but painful', says Hebrews 12:11. We are not asked to regard suffering as pleasant. Paul's thorn in the flesh was from Satan. It was evil. Evil is evil. Suffering is bad and God will eradicate it from His new creation.

2. Suffering is used by God. Second, God is at work in the midst of evil and suffering. Suffering is not a sign that the world is out of control. And *my* suffering is not a sign that *my* world is out of control. God has His purposes and they are for my good. Paul says: 'we know that in all things God works for the good of those who love him, who have been called according to his purpose.' And that purpose is that we 'be conformed to the image of his Son' (Rom. 8:28-29).

8. D. A. Carson, *How Long, O Lord? Reflections on Suffering and Evil*, 2nd. ed. (Nottingham: IVP, 2006), p. 65.

Hebrews 12:3-4 describes 'opposition from sinners' as part of our 'struggle against sin'. John Calvin says: 'When unbelievers persecute us in the Name of Christ we are striving against sin ... They are remedies to destroy sin.'[9] God uses sinful opposition to help us struggle against sin. In this way, God turns sin against sin!

We don't always need to work out God's purposes. We don't need to be able to say God sent *this* cancer to teach me *this* truth. Often God's purposes will remain hidden to us. Faith does not need to say *how* God is working to affirm *that* God is working through adversity.

In 1991 a drunk driver veered across the road into the car of Jerry Sittser and his family. His mother, wife and daughter were all killed — three generations in one moment. His book, *A Grief Disguised*, is an honest, often painful, reflection on his story. Yet Sittser writes: 'It is possible to live in and be enlarged by loss, even as we continue to experience it.'[10] He continues:

> Sometimes I wonder about how my own experience of loss will someday serve a greater purpose that I do not yet see or understand. My story may help to redeem a bad past, or it may bring about a better future. Perhaps my own family heritage has produced generations of absent and selfish fathers, and I have been given a chance to reverse that pattern. Perhaps people suffering catastrophic loss will someday look

9. John Calvin, *Hebrews and 1 & 2 Peter*, p. 189.

10. Jerry Sittser, *A Grace Disguised: How the Soul Grows through Loss*, expanded edition, (Grand Rapids, MI: Zondervan, 2004), p. 18.

to our family for hope and inspiration. I do not know. Yet I choose to believe that God is working towards some ultimate purpose, even using my loss to that end.[11]

So we don't need to label adversity as God's discipline in a *specific* way. God may be refining our faith in ways we cannot discern. Our 'job' is to endure patiently, all the time trusting in God's purposes in the present and God's promises for the future.

Thomas Boston, the early eighteenth-century Scottish pastor, wrote a book entitled *The Crook in the Lot*.[12] The title comes from Ecclesiastes 7:13: 'Consider what God has done: who can straighten what he has made crooked?' The subtitle is *The Sovereignty and Wisdom of God Displayed in the Afflictions of Men.* It is full of godly advice on understanding God's discipline. Boston says:

> No crook in the lot seems to be joyous, but grievous, making an unsightly appearance. Therefore men need to beware of giving way to their thoughts to dwell on the crook in their lot, and of keeping it too much in view .... Indeed, a Christian may safely take a steady and leisurely view of the crook in his lot in the light of the holy Word, which represents it as the discipline of the covenant. So faith will discover a hidden sightliness in it, under a very unsightly outward appearance; perceiving the suitableness of it to the

---

11. Jerry Sittser, *A Grace Disguised*, p. 199.

12. Thomas Boston, *The Crook in the Lot: The Sovereignty and Wisdom of God Displayed in the Afflictions of Men*, (London: Religious Tract Society, 1838).

infinite goodness, love, and wisdom of God, and to the real and most valuable interests of the party; by which means one comes to take pleasure, and that a most refined pleasure, in distress. But whatever the crook in the lot is to the eye of faith, it is not all pleasant to the eye of sense.[13]

In other words, how we view our afflictions makes all the difference. Afflictions really do look unpleasant to our senses. So we need to be careful not to think about them too much. But the Christian can and ought to look upon them with the eye of faith. We can see them as 'the discipline of the covenant' — the actions of 'the infinite goodness, love and wisdom of God'.

---

13. Thomas Boston, *The Crook in the Lot*, p. 9.

4.

Does Discipline Require a Change of Direction or Repentance From a Sin?

DOES DISCIPLINE REQUIRE A CHANGE OF DIRECTION?

Suppose someone embarks on a course of action. Perhaps they start a new job or a new ministry. And then let's suppose they find that they are often ill or they face opposition in their new ministry. Should they see these things as God's discipline and therefore as a sign that they should change direction? Is God making it clear that they made a wrong choice and have stepped out of His will?

Should we say, 'We're under Satanic attack so we must be doing something right!' or should we say, 'God has clearly closed the door on this opportunity.' How do we know whether we are called to endure hardship with patience or change direction?

In part this question assumes a wrong view of God's will. The Bible speaks of God's will in two ways. First, it speaks of God's sovereign will. Everything that happens does so in accordance with God's will. Nothing is outside His control. In this sense we can never step outside of God's will because there is nothing outside God's sovereign rule.

Second, the Bible speaks of God's moral will. God's word makes clear what behaviour is good and what behaviour is evil. 1 Thessalonians 4:3 says: 'It is God's will that you should be sanctified: that you should avoid sexual immorality', while 1 Thessalonians 5:18 exhorts us to 'give thanks in all circumstances; for this is God's will for you in Christ Jesus.' This moral will of God applies to all Christians at all times. And it is revealed to us in the Bible.

But people often assume a third sense of God's will — a specific will for my life. They assume it is God's will that I marry one person and not another, take one job and not another. They then get filled with angst trying to work out what God's specific will is in any situation. Is it God's will that I have toast for breakfast or porridge? How can I know?

What's good about this is that it reflects an assumption that God is intimately involved in our lives — which He is. But the fact is that the Bible never speaks of God's will in this way. Instead it calls on us to apply the teaching of the Bible to our lives with wisdom. There are a few examples in the New Testament of God directing people to change course (Acts 16:6-10). But these are the exception. God gives us the freedom to make choices within the boundaries of His moral will.

This means God's discipline never involves God telling us to change the direction of our lives — other than, of course, to live more in line with His *moral* will.

What's striking in Hebrews 12 is that the response to God's discipline is not described as a change of direction, but a call to 'endure' — to keep going in the same direction. Verse 7 says: 'Endure hardship as discipline.' This endurance is modelled on our Saviour. This teaching on God's discipline is prefaced with a call to consider Christ: 'Consider him who endured such opposition from sinners, so that you will not grow weary and lose heart' (v. 3). The goal of God's discipline is not a change of direction, but a change of attitude. The aim is 'holiness', 'righteousness' and 'peace' (vv. 10-11).

DOES DISCIPLINE REQUIRE REPENTANCE FROM A SPECIFIC SIN?

What about sin? Does discipline require repentance from a specific sin? This seems to be what is implied by the term 'chastens' in Hebrews 12:6. It's really important, as we've seen, to think of discipline as *more than* chastisement. It also includes training, education, pruning, experience. But it does include chastisement. We discipline children to change their behaviour.

So should we seek to correlate God's discipline to a specific sin of which we need to repent? The answer is *maybe, but not necessarily.*

The answer is maybe, because this is sometimes how God's discipline works. In 1 Corinthians 11 Paul describes a situation in which some Christians were attending the Lord's Supper without waiting for their poorer brothers and sisters. Possibly the poorer Christians were slaves who could only attend once their masters had released them from their day's work. So some in the church were eating and drinking to excess while others had nothing. Paul says: 'I hear that when you come together as a church, there are divisions among you, and to some extent I believe it' (1 Cor. 11:18). It's probably a reference to social distinctions. Some in Corinth were deliberately replicating and reinforcing the social distinctions within society. Their allegiance to their social class mattered more to them than their allegiance to the Christian family. Paul was horrified by this denial of their identity in Christ and therefore of the gospel. 'Don't you have homes to eat and drink in? Or do you despise the church of God by humiliating those who have nothing? What shall I say to you? Shall I praise you? Certainly not in this matter!' (1 Cor. 11:22). After reminding them of the true meaning of the Lord's Supper (11:23-27), he calls them to self-examination:

> Everyone ought to examine themselves before they eat of the bread and drink of the cup. For those who eat and drink without discerning the body of Christ eat and drink judgement on themselves. That is why many among you are weak and sick, and a number of you have fallen asleep. (1 Cor. 11:28-30)

God's discipline in Corinth took the form of illness and even death in response to the specific sin of despising the body of Christ in communion. So Paul called them to self-examination and repentance. Does discipline require repentance for a specific sin? In Corinth the answer was clearly, 'Yes'. Often God lets us live with the consequences of our sin. If you commit adultery then God's judgement may be a broken marriage. If you nurture bitterness then God's judgement may be a period in which you feel miserable. And sometimes God directly intervenes to judge, as He did in Corinth.

But God's discipline doesn't always work like this. Indeed, it doesn't normally work like this. The Bible is very clear that suffering is not normally the *direct* result of a specific sin. Jesus makes this clear in John 9:1-3. Jesus and his disciples meet a man born blind. A man born blind doesn't fit a view which assumes bad things always happen as a direct result of specific sins. So the disciples ask Jesus whether the man was born blind because of his sin or his parents' sin. John 9:3 says: 'Neither this man nor his parents sinned,' said Jesus, 'but this happened so that the works of God might be displayed in him.' Suffering and sickness in a general sense entered the world as a result of humanity's rebellion against God. But if you are diagnosed with cancer or you are made redundant or you are bereaved, this does not necessarily mean there is a sin in your life of which you need to repent.

Consider 1 Peter 4:16-17: 'If you suffer as a Christian, do not be ashamed, but praise God that you bear that name. For it is time for judgement to begin with God's household; and if it begins with us, what will the outcome be for those who do not obey the gospel of God?' The implication is that the suffering we experience as Christians is used by God to judge us. But in this case Peter's command is 'do not be ashamed'. In this case judgement cannot be a response to a specific sin because the Christians have nothing of which to be ashamed.

Remember, God's discipline includes training, education, pruning, formation as well as chastisement. Jerry Bridges concludes: 'It is true that God sometimes disciplines us because of our persistence in some particular sin …. But in the absence of specific and persistent sin, we can safely say that God's discipline addresses our overall character and the need to purge our character of its sinful tendencies.'[1]

This leaves us with the question, How can we know whether there is a specific sin of which we need to repent? It's complicated by the fact that we are all sinners. We all have sins that need repentance.

Let me suggest two things that will help.

1. THE SIN WILL BE PERSISTENT

God is not out to get us. He is not like a cruel school teacher who is waiting for us to make a mistake so He can pounce on us. God is our Father. He is not going to discipline us every time we sin. As we've said, His discipline is not punitive, but corrective. And

---

1. Jerry Bridges, 'The Blessing of Discipline', *Assured by God: Living in the Fullness of God's Grace*, ed. Burk Parsons, (Phillipsburg, NJ: P&R, 2006), p. 161.

that means He disciplines us when our lives need redirecting.

James begins his letter: 'Consider it pure joy, my brothers and sisters, whenever you face trials of many kinds, because you know that the testing of your faith produces perseverance' (1:2-3). So James is writing to people in the midst of hardship which God is using to produce perseverance. Yet James goes on to say: 'When tempted, no one should say, "God is tempting me." For God cannot be tempted by evil, nor does he tempt anyone; but each person is tempted when they are dragged away by their own evil desire and enticed' (1:13-14). In other words God is not trying to trip us up. He's not setting traps for us. He is in control of our circumstances — good and bad. But He is using them to bring us to maturity (James 1:4).

So don't be afraid. Don't worry that God will 'get' you every time you sin. Repentance should be daily. We sin. We say sorry. We turn back to God. We resolve to pursue God and His glory. We realign our affections. And what we find is that His mercies are new every morning (Lam. 3:22-23).

But if we neglect repentance, if our sin becomes persistent, if our hearts begin to harden then God may well intervene in love before we suffer a 'shipwreck with regard to the faith' (1 Tim. 1:19).

2. THE SIN WILL BE CLEAR

Disciplining dogs is hard work. You have to punish them the moment they do something wrong. If you wait then they won't make the correlation between their behaviour and your punishment. In the same way, discipline only works if people can see the connection between the sin and the chastisement.

God will not leave us in the dark. He won't leave us guessing. If God is disciplining us for a specific sin, it will be obvious. Even if we are blinded by our self-justification, other people will point it out to us (as Paul does to the church in Corinth in 1 Cor. 11).

So examine your heart. Is there a persistent sin that you are clearly committing? Then it may be that God's discipline is His call to repentance. Turn from your sin and discover afresh God's grace.

5.

Why Does God Discipline Us?

Why does God discipline us? 'God disciplines us for our good,' says Hebrews 12:10, 'that we may share in his holiness.' What does this involve? Let me suggest a number of facets to the holiness God works in us through His discipline.

1. GOD DISCIPLINES US TO TURN
US FROM SPECIFIC SINS

As we've already seen, God may discipline us to bring us to repentance for a specific sin. Paul Tripp talks about 'violent grace'. 'Our relationship with the Lord is never anything other than a relationship of grace …. But that grace that we have been given is not always comfortable grace.' Our problem, he explains, is that 'we all become way too comfortable with our sin ... so God blesses us with violent, uncomfortable grace.' No one wants to feel a burning sensation on their skin. But physical pain often alerts us that something is wrong. And so we withdraw our hands from the flame. In this case, pain prevents greater and lasting pain. 'In the same way, God's loving hammer of conviction is meant to break your heart, and the pain of heart you feel is meant to alert you to the fact that something is spiritually wrong inside of you.' He continues: 'God's grace isn't always comfortable because he isn't primarily working on our comfort; he's working on our character. With violent grace he will crush us because he loves us and is committed to our restoration, deliverance, and refinement. And that is something worth celebrating.'[1]

God especially uses suffering to expose sin in our hearts. Sinful desires can remain hidden in our hearts until those desires are thwarted and threatened. Then they erupt in sinful behaviour. Suffering is one of God's diagnostic tools to expose our selfishness and pride. Thomas Boston says: 'As the fire under the pot makes the scum rise up, appear on top, and run over; so the crook in the lot raises up from the bottom, and brings out such corruption as otherwise one could hardly imagine to be within.'[2]

---

1. Paul David Tripp, *Whiter Than Snow: Meditations on Sin and Mercy*, (Wheaton, IL: Crossway, 2008), pp. 34-5.

2. Thomas Boston, *The Crook in the Lot*, p. 29.

2. GOD DISCIPLINES US TO INCREASE OUR JOY IN CHRIST

God may use His discipline to wean us from our idols. There may be good things in our lives that have become idols. They matter more to us than God does. If we find delight in other things (success, possessions, approval) then the removal of these things will cause depression, anger, bitterness. If we are at the centre of our world then affliction will seem a terrible injustice. They may be good things in and of themselves, but God will not bless our idols. Instead, He will destroy them.

So sometimes in His discipline God is pulling open our fingers to release an idol from our grasp. It will be painful at the time. We will feel it as loss. But the good news is that God always offers us something better, for He offers us Himself. If we are open to God then this experience of loss will become an experience of gain. Thomas Boston again:

> Take God in Christ for and instead of that thing, the withholding or taking away of which from you makes the crook in your lot. There is never a crook which God makes in our lot, but it is in effect Heaven's offer of a blessed exchange to us; such as, *'Sell whatever you have — and you shall have treasure in heaven.'* In managing this exchange, God first puts out His hand, and takes away some earthly thing from us; and it is expected we put out our hand next and take some heavenly thing from Him instead of it, and particularly His Christ. Wherefore has God emptied your left hand of such and such an earthly comfort? Stretch out your

right hand to God in Christ; take Him in place of it, and welcome Him.[3]

<u>Suffering is an invitation to be satisfied in Christ</u>. This is why James and Peter can invite us to rejoice in suffering (James 1:2; 1 Pet. 1:6). God may use loss to bring us to the point where we can say with Paul: 'I consider everything a loss because of the surpassing worth of knowing Christ Jesus my Lord, for whose sake I have lost all things. I consider them garbage, that I may gain Christ' (Phil. 3:8).

3. GOD DISCIPLINES US TO WEAKEN DISTRACTING AFFECTIONS

Jesus said that in some people, 'the worries of this life, the deceitfulness of wealth and the desires for other things come in and choke the word, making it unfruitful' (Mark 4:19). So sometimes God removes our wealth and the other things we desire to make His word fruitful in our lives. Think of it as God clearing the undergrowth to create space for the flowers of holiness to blossom in our lives. Here's one example of how this might work. John Piper cites research that shows 'the richer we are, the smaller the percentage of our income we give to the church and its mission.'[4] Maybe God makes some of us poorer so we give more.

Or consider sickness. The nineteenth-century preacher Charles H. Spurgeon suffered a lot from illness. Yet

---

3. Thomas Boston, *The Crook in the Lot*, p. 49.

4. John Piper, 'Why God Appoints Suffering for His Servants,' *Suffering and the Sovereignty of God*, eds. John Piper and Justin Taylor, (Wheaton, IL: Crossway, 2006), p. 101.

he said: 'The greatest earthly blessing that God can give any of us is health, with the exception of sickness. Sickness has frequently been of more use to the saints of God than health has.' Why? Because 'trials lead us to the realities of the religion.'[5]

I have a friend who is an entrepreneur. There was a period when he was preoccupied with the business. The demands of cash flow meant his headspace was on the business, sometimes to the neglect of his family and church. He recognized the problem, but felt powerless to change. I tried to help, but there was little I could say that he didn't already know. Then he started a new joint venture with another company. It quickly ran into problems. It proved to be a difficult time — financially and relationally. Eventually he reached a point of detachment where he was happy to walk away. God used this experience to reshape his attitude to his main business. He began to feel a similar level of detachment. This was followed in God's providence by two months of orders that exceeded the orders he had received during the whole of the previous year and this helped alleviate cash flow problems. Through His discipline, God achieved the change of heart my friend needed which neither my friend, nor I as his pastor, could achieve through our efforts.

---

5. Cited (disapprovingly) in, 'Mr Spurgeon on Sickness,' *The Spectator*, 5 July 1890, pp. 18-19; archive.spectator.co.uk/article/5th-july-1890/18/mr-spurgeon-on-sickness.

Jerry Sittser says: 'Loss provides an opportunity to take inventory of our lives, to reconsider priorities, and to determine new directions.'[6] He writes:

> Deep sorrow often has the effect of stripping life of pretense, vanity, and waste. It forces us to ask basic questions about what is most important in life. Suffering can lead to a simpler life, less cluttered with non-essentials. It is wonderfully clarifying. That is why many people who suffer sudden and severe loss often become different people. They spend more time with their children or spouses, express more affection and appreciation to their friends, show more concern for other wounded people, give more time to a worthy cause, or enjoy more of the ordinariness of life.[7]

4. GOD DISCIPLINES US TO INCREASE OUR RELIANCE ON HIM

In 2 Corinthians 1:8-9 Paul describes the lesson he has learnt from his recent sufferings. 'We do not want you to be uninformed, brothers and sisters, about the troubles we experienced in the province of Asia. We were under great pressure, far beyond our ability to endure, so that we despaired of life itself. Indeed, we felt we had received the sentence of death. But this happened that we might not rely on ourselves but on God, who raises the dead' (2 Cor. 1:8-9). Paul's troubles pushed him beyond his ability to endure. And what did he discover there? A God who raises the dead.

---

6. Jerry Sittser, *A Grace Disguised*, p. 76.

7. Jerry Sittser, *A Grace Disguised*, p. 74.

Paul felt like a death sentence had been passed on him. But this didn't matter because God can raise the dead. Why did God allow Paul to undergo this trouble, pressure and despair? 'This happened that we might not rely on ourselves but on God.'

The fact is that when things are going well, I rely on myself and find joy in what I own. But when things are going badly, I rely on God and find joy in Him. Given this, the remarkable thing is that the Father doesn't send more afflictions into our lives! John Flavel writes: 'Let a Christian ... be but two or three years without an affliction, and he is almost good for nothing.'[8]

Jerry Sittser says: 'Loss forces us to see the dominant role our environment plays in determining our happiness. Loss strips us of the props we rely on for our well-being. It knocks us off our feet and puts us on our backs. In the experience of loss, we come to the end of ourselves.'[9] He goes on to describe what this looked like in his own experience:

> The tragedy pushed me towards God, even when I did not want him. And in God I found grace, even when I was not looking for it. As a single parent, I have reached the point of such frustration and fatigue that I have given up trying to be a perfect parent for my children and have instead invited God to be their parent through me.[10]

---

8. John Flavel, *The Mystery of Providence*, 1678, (Edinburgh: Banner of Truth, 1963), p. 202.

9. Jerry Sittser, *A Grace Disguised*, p. 89.

10. Jerry Sittser, *A Grace Disguised*, p. 90.

5. GOD DISCIPLINES US TO REFINE OUR FAITH

Peter invites his readers to rejoice even though they have had 'to suffer grief in all kinds of trials' (1 Pet. 1:6). Why are trials a reason to rejoice? He continues: 'These have come so that your faith — of greater worth than gold, which perishes even though refined by fire — may be proved genuine and may result in praise, glory and honour when Jesus Christ is revealed' (1 Pet. 1:7). God allows us to experience trials to refine our faith and prove our faith. The image is taken from gold smelting. The corrupted gold is heated until it melts. The dross then rises to the surface and can be poured off. What you are left with is purer gold. God disciplines us to purify our faith.

Judges 2:20–3:4 says God allowed the Canaanite nations to remain in the land 'to test all those Israelites who had not experienced any of the wars in Canaan.' As each new generation faced war, they were forced to trust in God for themselves. With an opposing army facing them across the battlefield, they had to choose between self-reliance or trust in God. They could not rely on second-hand faith.

A young person brought up in a Christian home will often share the beliefs of their parents. They will not remember a time when they were not involved in the life of the church. It is a natural thing for them to do. Faith for them has never been a choice they have had to make. It has, in a sense, been made for them by family and friends. But when suffering comes they face the enemy across the battlefield. Now they must decide. God uses trials so that their faith 'may be proved genuine'. Suffering may be the making of them as Christian men and women. Thomas Boston says:

> The crook in the lot is the great engine of Providence for making men appear in their true colours, discovering both their ill and their good. And if the grace of God is in them, it will bring it out, and cause it to display itself. It so puts the Christian to his shifts, that however it makes him stagger for awhile, yet it will at length evidence both the reality and the strength of grace in him.[11]

6. GOD DISCIPLINES US TO DISPLAY HIS POWER

At some point in his life, as we've already noted, Paul was given 'a thorn in my flesh, a messenger from Satan' (2 Cor. 12:7). We're not told exactly what it was. Perhaps that's to encourage us to make parallels with our own lives. Three times Paul pleaded with the Lord to take it away. But the Lord had other ideas. He wanted to use this thorn in the flesh to teach Paul. He said to Paul, 'My grace is sufficient for you, for my power is made perfect in weakness' (v. 9).

We so easily become self-reliant. We think we can cope with life. We think we can serve Christ well. We think we are coping and we are serving. But in fact we are coping with God's help and serving in His strength. So sometimes God uses suffering to make

---

11. Thomas Boston, *The Crook in the Lot*, p. 30.

us aware of our weakness so we become more aware of His power.

And that is a happy place to be. Paul's thorn in the flesh was clearly unpleasant. He pleaded for it to be taken away. But in the end it brought him gladness and delight. 'Therefore I will boast all the more gladly about my weaknesses, so that Christ's power may rest on me. That is why, for Christ's sake, I delight in weaknesses, in insults, in hardships, in persecutions, in difficulties. For when I am weak, then I am strong' (2 Cor. 12:9-10).

7. GOD DISCIPLINES US TO ENABLE US TO COMFORT OTHERS

Paul begins 2 Corinthians by describing God as 'the Father of compassion and the God of all comfort' because He 'comforts us in all our troubles' (1:3-4). Then Paul suggests a reason why God allows us to experience such troubles: 'So that we can comfort those in any trouble with the comfort we ourselves receive from God' (1:4). My friend Matt whose daughter has a brain tumour spoke to me recently of his increased compassion towards others and the opportunities his daughter's illness has brought. Another friend told me how having a difficult baby had made him much more sympathetic towards people he had previously regarded as 'moaning mums'. I'm convinced that my own struggles have increased my ability to pastor others.

Paul goes on: 'If we are distressed, it is for your comfort and salvation; if we are comforted, it is for your comfort, which produces in you patient endurance of the same sufferings we suffer' (1:6). We can be possessive about our suffering. We use it to excuse our behaviour, to warrant special treatment, to isolate ourselves, to make ourselves an exception — even though 1 Corinthians 10:13 says: 'the temptations in your life are no different from what others experience' (NLT). But Paul says our sufferings are not for us. They are for others. They are given by God so we can comfort others.

8. GOD DISCIPLINES US TO STRENGTHEN OUR HOPE

Romans 5 begins with Paul talking about the fruit of justification in our lives. We have peace with God. We have access to His grace. We rejoice in the hope of glory. But then he talks about suffering: 'Not only so, but we also glory in our sufferings, because we know that suffering produces perseverance; perseverance, character; and character, hope' (Rom. 5:3-4). It's a reminder that God's discipline is not punitive, for we have been justified so that we have peace with God and access to His grace. So our suffering is not a punishment. Instead it is character-building in the best sense of the word.

Suffering produces perseverance, character and hope. In the parable of the sower Jesus speaks of people who, 'when trouble or persecution comes because of the word, they quickly fall away' (Mark 4:17). But for those with true faith, trouble produces perseverance.

Character is what is produced as acts of faith and love become habitual. The 'keeping-going' of perseverance embeds itself in our lives. And the more we look to God in this life, the brighter the prospect of being with Him in the next life shines for us. Jesus says something similar in the Sermon on the Mount. He says we are blessed when people insult us and persecute us. 'Rejoice and be glad, because great is your reward in heaven' (Matt. 5:11-12). Suffering focuses our attention on our reward in heaven.

Hebrews 10:34 says: 'You suffered along with those in prison and joyfully accepted the confiscation of your property, because you knew that you yourselves had better and lasting possessions.' Imagine you lost all your property. How are you going to respond? You have a choice. You can be distraught at what you have lost. Or you can rejoice in what you have not lost — 'the better and lasting possessions' of heaven.

For the Puritan poet Anne Bradstreet this was not a theoretical choice. In 1630 Anne and her husband sailed to America to escape persecution. Life in the new world was hard and in 1666 fire destroyed their home. In a poem, Anne recalls her distress as the flames took hold and recounts the ruined possessions that she loved:

> Here stood that Trunk, and there that chest,
> There lay that store I counted best,
> My pleasant things in ashes lie
> And them behold no more shall I.

There is a real sense of loss expressed in this poem. But then she speaks to herself, reminding herself of the truth and calling on her heart to look to things above.

> Then straight I 'gin my heart to chide:
> And did thy wealth on earth abide?

She reminds herself that she has a home in heaven 'with glory richly furnished', paid for with the blood of Christ, 'a price so vast as is unknown'.

> The world no longer let me love;
> My hope and Treasure lies above.

9. GOD DISCIPLINES US TO PREPARE US FOR GLORY

In 2 Corinthians 4:17 Paul goes a step further. Not only does suffering direct our attention to our heavenly hope, our suffering actually prepares us for heaven. 'For our light and momentary troubles are achieving for us an eternal glory that far outweighs them all.' Does this mean we earn eternal life through our suffering? No, it is Christ who gives us eternal life. But our faithfulness in suffering does earn a reward from God. Those who have been faithful in suffering will be rewarded more than those who were unfaithful or suffered less. So our suffering in this life will enrich our experience of glory.

How does this work? Jonathan Edwards invites us to think of Christians as cups being dipped into the ocean of God's love. We will all be filled full so our joy will be complete. But some people will be larger cups, enlarged by their suffering in this life. As a result, they will be more full. Edwards says: 'There are different degrees of happiness and glory in heaven … Every one shall be perfectly satisfied. Every vessel that is cast into this ocean of happiness is full, though there are some vessels far larger than others.'[12]

Will those of us who are smaller vessels feel like we are missing out? No, because pure love will have replaced any envy. 'They will rejoice in their superior happiness, their love to them will be such that they will rejoice that they are happier than themselves; so that instead of having a damp to their own happiness, it will add to it.'[13] At the moment we all suffer from a degree of envy. But even in this life we can imagine how this might work. Think of a young woman who was brutally beaten and shamed for her faith in Christ. What will you think if she is honoured above you in heaven? Will you not rejoice that the faith that drove her sacrifice has been vindicated?

10. GOD DISCIPLINES US TO PRODUCE A HARVEST OF RIGHTEOUSNESS AND PEACE

Finally, let's return to Hebrews 12. Verse 11 says: 'No discipline seems pleasant at the time, but painful. Later on, however, it produces a harvest of righteousness and peace for those who have been trained by it.' Jerry Bridges says:

> We learn to love truly only when circumstances expose our inherent selfishness or only when we are placed in

---

12. Jonathan Edwards, *The Works of Jonathan Edwards*, (London: Ball, Arnold & Co., 1840), Volume 2, p. 902.

13. ibid.

close quarters with someone who is difficult to love. We learn true joy and peace only when we experience circumstances that in themselves tend to rob us of our joy and peace in the Lord. We learn patience only by being in the continual presence of someone whose actions try our patience. We learn to trust God only when he places us in circumstances in which we are forced to depend on him. All the admirable traits of Christian character then are formed and grown through the discipline of adversity.[14]

Reread this quote paying attention to the word 'only'. Feel its full force. There are some lessons we will *only* learn and some virtues we will *only* gain through the discipline of adversity. Richard Baxter says: 'Though the word and Spirit do the main work, yet suffering so unbolts the door of the heart, that the word hath easier entrance.'[15] Thomas Watson says: 'A sick-bed teaches more than a sermon.'[16]

---

14. Jerry Bridges, 'The Blessing of Discipline', p. 161.

15. Richard Baxter, *The Saints' Everlasting Rest*, 1650, (Welwyn: Evangelical Press, 1978), p. 246.

16. Thomas Watson, *All Things for Good*, p. 27.

6.

How Should We Respond to God's Discipline?

When we face adversity, it is first right and proper to ask God for our adversity to be removed. The fact that God uses suffering to discipline us doesn't mean we can't try to reduce suffering or pray for its removal. Thomas Boston says:

1. Pray for [relief], and pray in faith, believing that, for the sake of Jesus, you shall certainly obtain at length, and in this life too, if it is good for you; but without peradventure in the life to come …
2. Humble yourselves under it, as the yoke which the sovereign hand has laid on you …
3. Wait on patiently till the hand that made it mend it …. Leave the timing of the deliverance to the

> Lord; His time will at length, to conviction, appear
> the best, and it will not go beyond it.[1]

In the meantime, how should we respond to God's discipline? There is, as we have seen, a place for self-examination. God may use suffering to cause us to repent of a specific sin. But not necessarily so.

Hebrews 12 identifies a number of ways we should respond to God's discipline. We should 'not make light of the Lord's discipline' (12:5). We should 'not lose heart' (12:5). We should 'endure hardship as discipline' (12:7). And we should 'submit' to discipline as the act of a loving Father (12:9). 'There, strengthen your feeble arms and weak knees' (12:12).

There are two dangers here.

1. DON'T TREAT GOD'S DISCIPLINE LIGHTLY

We treat God's discipline lightly when we fail to see His hand in our hardship. This is so important. Too often we see hardship as a problem to be solved or a reality of life to put up with. We say things like: 'C'est la vie.' 'Whatever.' 'That's life.' But verse 7 says: 'Endure hardship *as discipline*.' In other words, when hardship comes think of it not only as hardship, but also as discipline.

It might be your life — your singleness or illness, perhaps. It might be your morning — the traffic jam in which you find yourself, perhaps. Whether it is a big life-shaping issue or a momentary inconvenience, think of it as something God intends for your holiness.

---

1. Thomas Boston, *The Crook in the Lot*, pp. 48-9.

Thomas Boston says: 'The considering of the crook in the lot as the work of God is a proper means to bring one to behave rightly under it.' It may well be, he argues, that a creature had a hand in our suffering. It may be the work of Satan or other people. But we need to look beyond these to see God's hand at work. Boston gives as an example, David. At one point in his life, David was forced out of Jerusalem by the rebellion of his son, Absalom. As he fled, a man named Shimei from Saul's family cursed him and pelted him with stones. One of David's men offers to go over and cut off Shimei's head. But David replies: 'Leave him alone; let him curse, for the LORD has told him to. It may be that the LORD will look upon my misery and restore to me his covenant blessing instead of his curse today' (2 Sam. 16:11-12). David sees beyond Shimei's curses to the hand of God. And this is his hope, for God is the God of covenant who has promised blessing to David.

In *A Grief Disguised*, Jerry Sittser emphasises that, while we can't always control what happens in our lives, we can choose how we respond. 'If we face loss squarely and respond to it wisely, we will actually become healthier people, even as we draw closer to physical death. We will find our souls healed, as they can only be healed through suffering.'[2]

The decision to face the darkness, even if it led to overwhelming pain, showed me that the experience of loss itself does not have to be the defining moment of our lives. Instead, the defining moment can be *our response* to the loss. It is not what happens *to* us that

---

2. Jerry Sittser, *A Grace Disguised*, p. 18.

matters as much as what happens *in* us. Darkness, it is true, had invaded my soul. but then again, so did light. Both contributed to my personal transformation.[3]

Sittser describes, for example, how the numbness of grief gave way to a new appreciation for the mundane responsibilities of life. 'I was struck by how wonderful ordinary life is. Simply being alive became holy to me.'[4]

This doesn't mean we can't try to reduce or remove suffering. But it does mean we should see God's hand in it and therefore seek to learn the lessons He has for us. It is possible to train children without them realising what is happening. God does shape us without us realising it is happening. But generally speaking, we will learn more if we are looking for God's lessons. So ask yourselves questions like:

- What can I learn?
- How can I lay hold of Christ?
- How should I turn to God in repentance?
- How should I turn to God in faith?

2. DON'T BE OVERWHELMED BY GOD'S DISCIPLINE

'Do not lose heart,' says verse 5. Sometimes we can feel overwhelmed by our problems. We may feel forsaken by God. But remember, God is not turning away from us, but inviting us to draw close to Him. Hardship is God's training regime and He knows what He's doing. 'No temptation has overtaken you except what is common to mankind. And God is faithful; he

---

3. Jerry Sittser, *A Grace Disguised*, p. 45.
4. ibid.

will not let you be tempted beyond what you can bear. But when you are tempted, he will also provide a way out so that you can endure it' (1 Cor. 10:13).

When does a normal and proper sorrow over affliction become ungodly joylessness? Thomas Boston answers: 'When it prevails so far as to unfit us for the duties either of our particular or Christian calling.'[5] Failing to see suffering as God's discipline, warns Boston, actually adds to our sorrow:

> Is it not wisdom then to make the best we may of what we cannot mend? Make a virtue then of necessity. What is not to be cured must be endured, and should be with a Christian resignation. An awkward carriage under it notably increases the pain of it. What makes the yoke gall our necks, but that we struggle so much against it, and cannot let it sit at ease on us … Impatience under the crook lays an overweight on the burden, and makes it heavier, while withal it weakens us, and makes us less able to bear it.[6]

Here is Boston's advice on how we should respond to God's discipline:

1. Consider it as the work of your God in Christ. This is the way to sprinkle it with Gospel-grace, and so to make it tolerable. The discerning of a Father's hand in the crook will take out much of the bitterness of it, and sugar the pill to you. For this cause it will be necessary,

---

5. Thomas Boston, *The Crook in the Lot*, p. 52.
6. Thomas Boston, *The Crook in the Lot*, p. 53.

(1.) Solemnly to take God for your God, under your crook.

(2.) In all your encounters with it, resolutely to believe and claim your interest in Him.

2. Enlarge the consideration with a view of the Divine relations to you, and the Divine attributes. Consider it, being the work of your God, the work of your Father, elder Brother, Head, Husband, etc., who, therefore, surely consults your good. Consider His holiness and justice, showing He does not wrong you; His mercy and goodness, that it is not worse; His sovereignty, that may silence you; His infinite wisdom and love, that may satisfy you in it.

3. Consider what a work of His it is, how it is a convincing work, for bringing sin to remembrance: a correcting work, to chastise you for your follies, a preventing work, to hedge you up from courses of sin you would otherwise be apt to run into; a trying work, to discover your state, your graces, and corruption; a weaning work, to wean you from the world and fit you for heaven.

4. In all your considerations of it in this manner look upward for His Spirit to render them effectual. Thus may you behave Christianly under it, till God make it even either here or in heaven.[7]

One thing we can do that simultaneously stops us making light of God's discipline and being overwhelmed by it is to *thank* Him for it. Thanking God involves us

---

7. Thomas Boston, *The Crook in the Lot*, pp. 64-5.

taking discipline seriously as a means of producing holiness. And thanking God means we see it as a gift from a gracious Father. Jerry Bridges says:

> Our natural tendency, especially in the ordinary difficulties of life, is to fret and fume and to succumb to feelings of frustration. However, believing that he will use this situation for our good so that we may share in his holiness, by an act of will we thank God for what he is doing in our lives through the particular circumstance.[8]

A WORD OF ENCOURAGEMENT

God's discipline is one of those topics we don't like to think about. In some ways, it's not a pleasant topic as the writer of Hebrews acknowledges: 'No discipline seems pleasant at the time, but painful' (12:11). And yet the same writer introduces his teaching on God's discipline by describing it as 'a word of encouragement'. God's discipline is a truth that should encourage and excite us. Why?

1. Because discipline is a sign that God is our Father (Heb. 12:5-9).
2. Because God uses His discipline in order that we may share in His holiness (Heb. 12:10-11).

I like to think of it like this. Each day when I wake up, God has planned a whole programme of activities and experiences for me. Some of those experience will be

---

8. Jerry Bridges, 'The Blessing of Discipline', p. 165.

happy. Some will be painful. But they are all tailor-made to produce in me holiness, righteousness and peace. And they are all designed by my Father. He has only my good at heart. Each one is an act of love, however unpleasant it may seem at the time. I can go through the day knowing that everything that happens is part of His training regime or His work-experience programme to produce in me righteousness and peace. This transforms my attitude to the day. I get up each morning wondering what lessons God has in store for me.

7.

John Flavel on Nine Ways of Keeping Your Heart Under Affliction

In his book *Saint Indeed* the Puritan preacher John Flavel takes as his starting point Proverbs 4:23: 'Keep thy heart with all diligence, for out of it are the issues of life' (KJV). Our behaviour and emotions are always an expression of the desires of our hearts. So how we respond to the circumstances of our lives is determined by what's going on in our hearts. This makes keeping our hearts set on God a matter of primary importance. Flavel defines this as 'the diligent and constant use and improvement of all holy means and duties, to preserve the soul from sin, and maintain its sweet and free communion with God.' After some general advice, Flavel considers twelve case studies. In the second of these he offers nine ways of keeping your heart under great affliction.[1] This is reproduced below with updated words, spellings and word orders as well as added headings. It's a great example of Puritan pastoral wisdom.

The second special season in the life of a Christian that requires particular diligence to keep the heart is *the time of adversity.* When providence frowns upon you, and blasts your outward comforts, then look to your hearts. Keep them with all diligence from grumbling against God or fainting under His hand. For troubles, though sanctified, are still troubles. Even sweet-briar and holy thistle have their prickles. Jonah was a good man, and yet how petulant was his heart under affliction? Job was the mirror of patience, yet how was his heart unsettled by trouble? You will find it as hard to get a composed spirit under great afflictions as it is to fix quick silver. O the agitation and turmoil they cause even in the best hearts!

So our second case is this: *How a Christian under great afflictions may keep his heart from grumbling or despondency under the hand of God.* There are nine special helps I shall offer to keep your heart in these circumstances.

---

1. An extract from 'Saint Indeed or the Great Work of a Christian Explained and Applied', *Works,* Volume 5, 1820; reprinted, (Edinburgh: Banner of Truth, 1968), pp. 441-6. Also published as *Keeping the Heart: How to Maintain your Love for God* (Ross-shire: Christian Focus Publications, 2012).

1. GOD IS PURSUING HIS LOVING PLANS

The first truth to work into your hearts is this: *By these unwelcome providences, God is faithfully pursuing the great design of His electing love for the souls of His people; and He orders all these afflictions as a means sanctified to that end.* Afflictions do not happen by chance, but by counsel (Job 5:6; Eph. 1:11). By this counsel of God they are ordained as means of much spiritual good to saints 'By this shall the iniquity of Jacob be purged' (Isa. 27:9). 'God disciplines us for our good, in order that we may share in his holiness' (Heb. 12:10). 'All things work together for our good' (Rom. 8:28). They are God's workmen upon our hearts to pull down pride and earthly security. And being so, their nature is changed. They are turned into blessings and benefits. 'It is good for me that I have been afflicted' (Ps. 119:71). So you have no reason to quarrel with God. Rather you should marvel that God should concern Himself so much with your good, that He will use any means to accomplish it. Paul could bless God, if by any means, he might attain the resurrection of the dead (Phil. 3:11). 'My brethren,' says James, 'count it all joy when you fall into divers temptations' (James 1:2-3). My Father is about a design of love on my soul, and should I be angry with Him? All that He does is in pursuance of, and in reference to, some eternal glorious ends upon my soul. It is my ignorance of God's design that makes me quarrel with Him! He says to you in this case, as to Peter, 'You do not realise now what I am doing, but later you will understand' (John 13:7).

2. GOD HAS BOUND HIMSELF TO US IN COVENANT LOVE

Though God has reserved to Himself the freedom to afflict His people, yet He has tied up His own hands by His promise never to take away His loving-kindness from them. Can I look that Scripture in the face with a grumbling, discontented spirit? 'I will be his father, and he shall be my son; if he commit iniquity, I will chasten him with the rod of men, and with the stripes of the children of men: nevertheless, my mercy shall not depart away from him' (2 Sam. 7:14 KJV). O my heart, my haughty heart! Should you be discontented when God has given you the whole tree, with all the clusters of comfort growing on it, just because He suffers the wind to blow down a few leaves? Christians have two sorts of goods: the goods of the throne and the goods of the footstool. If God has secured the goods of the heavenly throne, never let my heart be troubled at the loss of the goods of the earthly footstool. If He had cut off His love or broken His covenant with my soul, I would have reason to be cast down. But He has not done this, nor can He do it.

3. THE ONE WHO AFFLICTS US IS OUR FATHER

A marvellously effective way to keep the heart from sinking under affliction is *to call to mind that your own Father has organised them.* Not a creature moves its hand or tongue against you, but by His permission. Suppose the cup be a bitter cup. Yet it is the cup which your Father has given you to drink. So can you suspect poison to be in that cup which He delivers to you? Foolish man, put the case to your own heart and consult with your own compassion. Could you find it in your heart to give your child that which would hurt and undo him? No, you would as soon hurt yourself as him. 'If you, then, though you are evil, know how to give good gifts to your children,' how much more does God? (Matt. 7:11). The consideration of His nature as a God of love, pity and tender mercies or of His relation to you as a father, husband, friend, might be security enough, even if He had not spoken a word to quiet you in this situation. And yet you have His word too: 'I will not harm you' (Jer. 25:6). You lie too near His heart for Him to hurt you. Nothing grieves Him more than your groundless and unworthy suspicions of His designs. Consider a faithful, tender-hearted physician who has studied the case of his patient and prepared the most excellent remedies to save his life. Would it not grieve him to hear his patient cry out, 'He has undone me! He has poisoned me,' because the operation gripes and pains him?

4. GOD LOVES YOU WHETHER YOU ARE HIGH OR LOW

God esteems you as much in a low as in a high condition; and therefore it need not trouble you so much to be made low. Indeed, He manifests more of His love, grace and tenderness in the time of affliction than prosperity. Just as God did not at first choose you because you were high, so He will not forsake you because you are low. Men may look on you with embarrassment and alter their respects, as your condition is altered. When providence has blasted your estates, your summer friends may grow strange, fearing you may be troublesome to them. But will God do so? No, no. 'Never will I leave you; never will I forsake you' (Heb. 13:5). If indeed adversity and poverty could bar you from access to God, it would be a sad condition. But you may go to God as freely as ever. 'My God,' says the church, 'will hear me' (Micah 7:7). Poor David, when stripped of all earthly comforts, could still encourage himself in the Lord his God, and why cannot you? Suppose your husband or child had lost all at sea and should come to you in rags. Could you deny your relationship to them or refuse to welcome them? If you would not, much less will God. Why then are you so troubled? Though your condition be changed, your Father's love and esteem are not changed.

5. GOD USES AFFLICTION TO PROTECT US FROM TEMPTATION

And what if by the loss of outward comforts, God will preserve your souls from the ruining power of temptation? Surely then, you will have little cause to sink your hearts by such sad thoughts about them? Are not these earthly enjoyments the things that make men shrink and warp in times of trial? For the love of these, many have forsaken Christ in such an hour. 'He went away sorrowful, for he had great possessions' (Matt. 19:22). And if this be God's design, what have I done in quarrelling with Him about it? We see how mariners in a storm can throw overboard rich bales of silk and precious things to preserve the vessel and their lives with it. And everyone says they act prudently. We know it is usual for soldiers in a besieged city to batter down or burn the fairest buildings outside the walls to prevent the enemy sheltering during the siege. And no man doubts but it is the wise thing to do. Those who have gangrene in their legs or arms can willingly stretch them out to be cut off. And they not only thank, but pay the surgeon for his pains. And must God alone be grumbled at for casting over what will sink you in a storm? For pulling down that which would give an advantage to your enemy in the siege of temptation? For cutting off what would endanger your everlasting life? O inconsiderate, ungrateful man! Are not these things for which you grieve the very things that have ruined thousands of souls? Well, what Christ does in this, you know not now, but afterwards you may understand.

6. GOD USES AFFLICTION TO ANSWER OUR PRAYERS
It would much calm the heart under adversity, to consider, *that God by such humbling providences may be accomplishing that for which you have long prayed and waited.* And should you be troubled at that? Christian, you may have many prayers before God that depend on such accounts as these: that He would keep you from sin; that He would reveal to you the emptiness and insufficiency of the creature; that He would kill and mortify your lusts; that your heart may never find rest in any enjoyment but Christ. It may be that, by such humbling and impoverishing strokes, God is fulfilling your desire to be kept from sin. 'I will block her path with thorn bushes' (Hosea 2:6). Do you want to see the futility of trusting in created things? Your affliction is a fair mirror to discover it. For the futility of created things is never so effectually and clearly discovered as in our own experience of it. Do you want your sinful corruption mortified? This is the way. For now God takes away the food and fuel that maintained them. For as prosperity

gave birth to them and fed them, so adversity, when sanctified, is a means to kill them. Do you want your heart to rest nowhere but in the bosom of God? What better way can you imagine providence accomplishing your desire than by pulling from under your head that soft pillow of creature-delights on which you previously rested? And yet you fret at this, peevish child, trying your father's patience? If He delays answering your prayers, you say He regards you not. But He is answering the scope and main end of your prayers, just not in the way you expected. Yet you quarrel with Him for that as if, instead of answering, He were frustrating all your hopes and aims. Is it not enough that God is so gracious to do what you desire, but you must be so impudent as to expect Him to do it in the way which you prescribe?

7. GOD HAS PURPOSES IN YOUR AFFLICTION WHICH YOU CANNOT SEE

Again, it may calm your heart if you consider *that in these troubles, God is about that work which, if you saw its design, your soul would rejoice.* Our eyes are misted over with much ignorance. So we are not able to discern how particular providences work towards God's end. And therefore, like Israel in the wilderness, we often murmur because providence leads us about in a howling desert where we are exposed to difficulties. Yet God led them, as He is now leading us, 'by a straight way to a city where they could settle' (Psalm 107:7). If only you could see how God in His secret counsel has exactly laid the whole plot and design of your salvation, even to the smallest means and circumstances. 'This way and by these means such a one shall be saved, and by no other.' 'Such a number of afflictions I appoint for this man, at this time, and in this order, and they shall befall him thus, and thus they shall work for him.' Can you, I say, discern the admirable harmony of divine plans, their mutual relations to each other, together with the general relationship and influence they all have on the final end? If you could, then, of all the conditions in the world, you would choose that in which you are now. Providence is like a careful piece of tapestry, made of a thousand scraps. We do not know what to make of a single scrap. But put together, and stitched up in an ordered way, they represent a beautiful history to the eye. As God works all things according to the counsel of His own will, so that counsel of God has ordained this as the best way to bring about your salvation. 'This one has a proud heart, so many humbling providences I appoint for him.' 'This one has an earthly heart, so many impoverishing providences for him.' If you could only see this, then I need say no more to support the most dejected heart.

8. OUR DISCONTENT HARMS US MORE THAN OUR AFFLICTIONS

Further, it would be very conducive to the settlement of your hearts to consider *that, by fretting and discontent, you do yourselves more injury than all the afflictions you lie under could do.* Your own discontent is that which arms your troubles with a sting. It is you that makes your burden heavy by struggling under it. If you would just lie quiet under the hand of God, your condition would be much easier and sweeter than it is. The impatient patient makes the physician cruel. This makes God lay on more strokes, as a father will on a stubborn child who rejects correction. Affliction is a pill which, being wrapped up in patience and quiet submission, may be easily swallowed. But discontent chews the pill and so embitters the soul. God throws away some comfort which He saw would hurt you, and you will throw away your peace after it. He shoots an arrow which sticks in your clothes. It was never intended to hurt, but only to frighten you away from sin. But you thrust the arrow onward by your despondency and discontent so that your heart is pierced.

9. YOUR PRESENT CONDITION IS BETTER THAN THE HELL YOU DESCRIBE

Lastly, if after all this your heart still refuses to be comforted or quieted, then consider one thing more. If seriously pondered, this will undoubtedly do the work. And that is this: *Compare the condition you are now in (and are so dissatisfied with) with the condition others are in and which you yourself deserve to be in.* Others are roaring in flames, howling under the scourge of vengeance. And among them I deserve to be. O my soul! Is this hell? Is my condition as bad as the condition of the damned? O what thousands now in hell would give to change conditions with me! The Duke of Conde, [a sixteenth-century French Protestant], chose poverty for the sake of true religion. One day an Italian lord saw him and pitied him. Out of tenderness the Italian lord urged the Duke to look after himself. The good Duke answered, 'Sir, don't be troubled, and don't think I have no provision for my comforts. For I've sent a herald before me who's preparing my lodgings and he will ensure I'm royally entertained.' The lord asked him who was his herald. He answered, 'The knowledge of myself, and the consideration of what I deserve for my sins, which is eternal torment. And when with this knowledge I arrive at my lodging, however I find it, I always think it is better than I deserve.' 'Why should the living complain?' (Lam. 3:39).

And thus the heart may be kept from despondency or grumbling under adversity.

 CROSSLANDS

Crosslands aims to provide excellent in-context theological training and resources to churches and church leaders in the UK, Europe and 10:40 window.

We are a new kind of entity, which we call a *flexicademy*™ — not residential training nor pure distance learning, but flexible learning and rigorous training for students where they live and minister. In other words, 'Gospel training when and where you need it'.

We offer a range of courses at seminary-level (for leaders and trainee leaders) and foundation-level (for congregation members, elders and interns). We're also starting to develop entry-level materials for new Christians.

Find out more at www.crosslands.training

More books by Tim Chester ...

Porterbrook

Crown of Thorns

Connecting Kingdom and Cross

Tim Chester

ISBN 978-1-7819-1614-8

Crown of Thorns

Connecting Kingdom and Cross

TIM CHESTER

Within evangelicalism today it can sometimes seem there are two competing versions of the gospel. There is the gospel of the kingdom with its focus on God's plan to restore the world. And there is the gospel of the cross with its focus on the offer of forgiveness. These two emphases create contrasting models of discipleship and mission.

In Crown of Thorns Tim Chester shows how these two gospels are really one gospel — the message of the King who establishes justice in a surprising way.

Is the gospel about the coming of the kingdom of God and its implications for social justice in this world? Or does it centre on the cross, dealing only with personal salvation and the need for forgiveness? ... Chester employs clear exegesis of biblical passages to help build his case, particularly from Mark's Gospel. He writes in a lively style and has produced a helpful little book. It will be particularly useful for young believers and those just beginning as preachers. Its brevity will enhance its appeal. I have pleasure in commending it.
Evangelical Times

The
Ascension:
Humanity in
the Presence
of God

Tim Chester &
Jonny Woodrow

ISBN 978-1-7819-1144-0

The Ascension

Humanity in the Presence of God

TIM CHESTER & JONNY WOODROW

Who is this ascended Jesus? He is King, Priest and man and is still at work. Ultimately He is humanity in the presence of God. Here we discover how we are a part of the Ascension. With the Spirit's enlightening we can begin to understand the Ascension. Tim Chester introduces us to this important doctrine.

The writers show us the Bible's answers to these questions and many more. If you have ever wondered why the ascension is critical to being a disciple of Jesus or why it wasn't just a bad strategy by God that removed the main evidence for Christianity, you will find plenty of help here.

Marcus Honeysett
Director of Living Leadership and author

Chester and Woodrow have given us a gift that will lift our eyes from this temporal horizon to the steppes of eternal joys of our High Priest in heaven.

Eric C. Redmond
Executive Pastoral Assistant and Bible Professor in Residence New Canaan Baptist Church, Washington, D.C.
Council Member, The Gospel Coalition

Christian Focus Publications

Our mission statement –

STAYING FAITHFUL

In dependence upon God we seek to impact the world through literature faithful to His infallible Word, the Bible. Our aim is to ensure that the Lord Jesus Christ is presented as the only hope to obtain forgiveness of sin, live a useful life and look forward to heaven with Him.

Our books are published in four imprints:

CHRISTIAN
FOCUS

Popular works including biographies, commentaries, basic doctrine and Christian living.

CHRISTIAN
HERITAGE

Books representing some of the best material from the rich heritage of the church.

MENTOR

Books written at a level suitable for Bible College and seminary students, pastors, and other serious readers. The imprint includes commentaries, doctrinal studies, examination of current issues and church history.

CF4•K

Children's books for quality Bible teaching and for all age groups: Sunday school curriculum, puzzle and activity books; personal and family devotional titles, biographies and inspirational stories – because you are never too young to know Jesus!

Christian Focus Publications Ltd,
Geanies House, Fearn, Ross-shire,
IV20 1TW, Scotland, United Kingdom.
www.christianfocus.com
blog.christianfocus.com